The Prophetic Mantle

The Prophetic Mantle

*

The Gift of Prophecy and Prophetic Operations in the Church Today

Written by: Roderick L. Evans

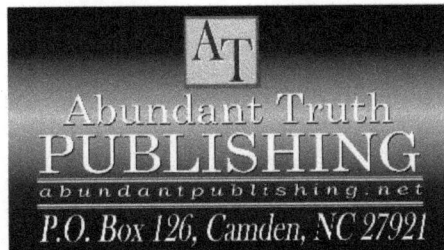

Abundant Truth
PUBLISHING
abundantpublishing.net
P.O. Box 126, Camden, NC 27921

The Prophetic Mantle

The Gift of Prophecy and Prophetic Operations in the Church Today

Front & Back Cover Designs by Abundant Truth Publishing U.S.A. All Rights Reserved.

Abundant Truth Publishing
an imprint of Abundant Truth International Ministries

For information address:
Abundant Truth International
P.O. Box 126
Camden, NC 27921

ISBN: 978-1-60141-290-4

Printed in the United States of America

Contents

Preface

The gift of prophecy is an important gift in the Church. God uses this gift to reveal His mind and heart to His people. However, there are individuals because of immaturity, pride, and other various reasons that have mishandled the use of this gift. This has caused misery in the lives of some believers.

I wrote this book to clarify the purpose of the gift of prophecy and prophetic ministry. This work comes from a desire to see the Body of Christ grounded in the function of the prophetic gift. I, personally, have been blessed by this gift and want to see others trust in its operation.

Roderick L. Evans

Introduction

Controversy over the gifts and ministries of the Spirit has abounded for centuries. Various scholars have taught that there was a cessation of the gifts. More specifically, they affirm that the gifts of the Spirit as listed in I Corinthians 12 are no longer in operation nor valid. However, in recent years, a resurgence of the operation and demonstration of the gifts has occurred. Traditional and Non-traditional churches, alike, have experienced the visitation of God through the Holy Spirit.

Since the emergence and acceptance of the gifts of the Holy Spirit, various authors have written concerning this phenomenon. In spite of this, many in the Church, presently, do not understand the functions and operations of the gifts. One gift among these that cause great controversy is the gift of prophecy. Even in organizations and denominations that consider the gifts valid today, comprehension is oftentimes elementary.

Where there is no clear understanding, individuals become vulnerable to deception and error. Since the gift of prophecy is an awesome gift, there are individuals in the Church who desire to have this gift. There are men and women who know they do not have this gift, yet they pursue it. They lust after the respect that men have for those who possess this gift. This has produced erroneous prophetic ministry in the Church. Many lives have been negatively influenced. Misery was a product of these mishaps in ministry.

The focus of this book is to bring clarity to the gift of prophecy, prophetic operations, and to the pitfalls associated with prophetic ministry. This information will help individuals to rediscover the purpose of the prophetic gift in the Church. It is our hope that believers will develop a greater respect and appreciation for the inspiration, revelation, and power of the Holy Spirit in the Body of Christ.

1

The Prophetic Gift

Thus saith the Lord." This is an expression that some believers cannot wait to hear and an expression that some despise. In spite of these feelings, God has placed this gift in the body of Christ. It is not only reserved for those who are prophets, but for any believer whom the Spirit will use. It is a widely publicized gift, but many are still confused about its use, function, and purpose.

The Greek word for 'to prophesy' is 'propheteuo.' It means to foretell events and speak under divine inspiration. This means that the source of prophecy is God.

No one can prophesy except the Lord gives the revelation. Prophetic ministry is interwoven throughout the Old Testament. There are different Hebrew words used to describe prophecy. Two prevalent words are 'Raba' and 'Nataf.' Each describes a different aspect of prophecy. Raba means to pour forth or spurt. This speaks of the oftentimes spontaneous method in which prophecy is received and administered.

Numerous accounts tell of the prophetic spirit coming suddenly on individuals to deliver God's message. Nataf means to drop or rain heavily. This speaks of the source of the prophecy. This demonstrates that the prophetic word comes from God above, like the rain does from the sky.

The Gift of Prophecy

In its simplest form to prophesy means to speak for God under divine inspiration. When someone gives a word of prophecy, it must be a "now" word; meaning, the word should be coming fresh from God. Some things that we call prophecy are really the word of knowledge or the word of wisdom in operation.

Prophecy can be predictive, but this is not its main function. Prophecy is designed to help the believer know what is the mind and heart of God. Prophecy serves as a testimony of the Lord Jesus Christ being in the midst of His people (Revelation 19:10).

Paul instructed the believers to covet the best gifts, especially prophecy. Prophecy is a direct word from the Lord. It does not come from intuition, feelings, or thought. It comes from the Spirit of the Lord.

Whether through a prophet or layman, prophecy always comes with a purpose. In the most basic terms, prophecy comes with edification, exhortation, and comfort.

> *But one who prophesies speaks to men for edification, exhortation, and consolation. One who speaks in a tongue edifies himself; but one who prophesies edifies the church. (I Corinthians 14:3-4 NASV)*

Edify means to erect, build, or construct. When a word of prophecy is spoken, it should help to build up or strengthen believers in their walk with the Lord. Exhort means to encourage or provoke an action. Many associate exhortation with encouragement only.

Though this is true, but there is another side to exhortation. Sometimes, exhortation is given that the people of God may repent and change their ways. The prophetic message may contain elements of rebuke through exhortation.

Comfort means to succor, help, or soothe. Oftentimes, the word of prophecy comes with a demonstration of the love and care of God for His people. This causes believers to be comforted in their trials, tests, and struggles. Whenever a word of prophecy is given, it should accomplish at least one of these three.

The Prophetic Anointing

There are individuals in the Church who are not prophets, but there is a definite prophetic touch on their lives and ministries. These individuals are said to possess a prophetic anointing. How does this differ from someone who has the gift of prophecy?

In simple terms, the person who has the gift of prophecy will prophesy on occasion. However, an individual with a prophetic anointing will prophesy frequently as they minister to the Body of Christ. Possessing a prophetic anointing does not place one in the office of the prophet, but it does make them one of the sons (or daughters) of the prophets. In the scriptures, the sons of the prophets would prophesy, but not with the same level of influence as those called to the prophetic office such as Jeremiah, Elijah, Ezekiel, Joel, and others.

The prophetic anointing is seen oftentimes in believers who are called to the five-fold ministry. They will operate in their respective offices while exercising prophetic insight and authority. The prophetic anointing adds a depth and dimension to their ministries.

In addition, one does not have to be called to a ministry office to possess a prophetic anointing. These individuals are strategically placed in the Body of Christ that all may be partakers of the prophetic ministry. Individuals who possess a prophetic anointing will prophesy frequently. They will have dreams and visions consistently. In addition, they will be able to recognize and discern the word of the Lord for a particular situation.

The Prophetic Office

Every believer is a candidate for the gift of prophecy. However, what makes the ministry of the prophet different from other believers who prophesy? The answer to this question is simple.

The prophecy of the prophet will provide direction, give insight into purpose, rebuke, correct, and reveal future events in God's eternal purpose. This is in addition to edification, exhortation, and comfort. When the prophet ministers, the prophecies will be of greater depth, dimension, and clarity.

The prophet's ministry is foundational. The prophecies of the prophet will often include revelation concerning the will of God for an individual's life and ministry. Also, the prophetic ministry of the prophet will reveal areas of spiritual weakness; including areas of spiritual warfare. The prophet's revelation will be of a greater strength even of those who possess a prophetic anointing.

The Spirit of Prophecy

The greatest expression of prophecy is not in the gift of prophecy or in the prophetic anointing. It is in the spirit of prophecy. The scriptures reveal that the spirit of prophecy is the testimony of Jesus.

And I fell at his feet to worship him. And he said unto me, See thou do it not: I am thy fellowservant, and of thy brethren that have the testimony of Jesus: worship God: for the testimony of Jesus is the spirit of prophecy. (Revelation 19:10)

In the Book of Revelation, the testimony of Jesus was the affirmation of Christ's death, burial, resurrection, and supremacy. The spirit of prophecy represents the Church's proclamation to the world of Christ. How does this affect the local assembly?

When the spirit of prophecy is manifested in an assembly, any believer present will able to prophesy even if he/she does not have the gift of prophecy or a prophetic anointing. The spirit of prophecy comes to unify the Church so that the Church represents one voice to any unbelievers that are present.

Paul alludes to the spirit of prophecy in his letter

to the Corinthians.

> *But if all prophesy, and there come in one that believeth not, or one unlearned, he is convinced of all, he is judged of all. (I Corinthians 14:24)*

The only time all believers will be able to prophesy at once is when the spirit of prophecy is present.

Paul writes that the unbeliever is judged of all. This means that the unbeliever is faced with the reality of God. This is how the spirit of prophecy is Jesus' testimony. The unbeliever will not be able to deny God's existence through its manifestation.

> *And thus are the secrets of his heart made manifest; and so falling down on his face he will worship God, and report that God is in you of a truth. (I Corinthians 14:25)*

Now that we have discussed the different aspects of prophecy, we have created a diagram on this page, showing the different stages in prophecy. The

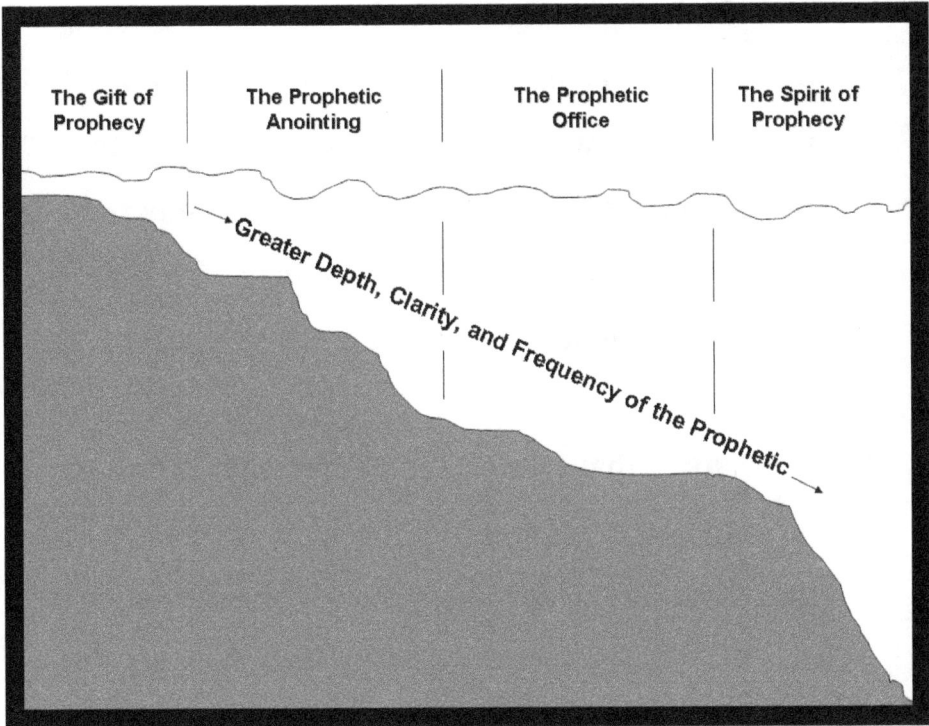

The Gift of Prophecy	The Prophetic Anointing	The Prophetic Office	The Spirit of Prophecy

Greater Depth, Clarity, and Frequency of the Prophetic

prophetic progression from the gift of prophecy to the spirit of prophecy is comparable to an ocean's geography. The further one goes out, the deeper the water becomes. Prophecy manifests in a similar manner. The illustration of the ocean is given also to provide the basis for a general warning regarding

11

the prophetic. One must remember to operate in the measure of the prophetic that God gives them.

In the diagram, the further one goes out, the deeper the water becomes. If one operates beyond his measure, he will drown; that is, go into error and kill the prophetic that is within him. Remember, do not try to operate in a prophetic realm for which God has not called you.

Now that we have addressed what is prophecy, a clear view of what is not prophecy is obtainable. In the next chapter, we will examine the ways in which prophecy is delivered; that is, the prophetic vehicle.

2

The Prophetic Vehicle

The word of prophecy comes to believers in different ways. No one way is better than the other. God operates in variety. Therefore, He uses numerous ways to bring His word to us. The manner in which God brings His word to us is referred to as the prophetic vehicle.

vehicle - a medium through which something is expressed, achieved, or displayed; a means of carrying or transporting something.

God uses different means to bring His words to
His people for ministry.

Paul spoke of the diversity in the operation and function of the gifts in I Corinthians 12.

Now there are diversities of gifts, but the same Spirit. And there are differences of administrations, but the same Lord. And there are diversities of operations, but it is the same God which worketh all in all. But the manifestation of the Spirit is given to every man to profit withal. (I Corinthians 12:4-7)

Just as there are different vehicles in the world, there are different ways God will impart prophetic revelation. The most common prophetic vehicles will be explored.

Voice of the Lord

The widely used prophetic vehicle is the voice of the Lord. When we state the voice of the Lord, we speak of God speaking to our spirit through the Holy Ghost. God commonly brings prophetic words to His people through direct communication. Once the individual hears the Lord, they are responsible to deliver the message that He spoke.

> *...and he that hath my word, let him speak my word faithfully. What is the chaff to the wheat? saith the Lord. (Jeremiah 23:28b)*

Contrary to popular belief, God will speak to us most often in our spirits. The Holy Spirit will speak to us what God is saying. Jesus said that this is a sign of His coming.

> *Howbeit when he, the Spirit of truth, is come, he will guide you into all truth: for he shall not speak of himself; but whatsoever he shall hear, that shall he speak: and he will shew you things to come. (John 16:13)*

Some believe that the prophets of Old heard God's

audible voice. However, many of the accounts do not state this. There are times when God's words will come to us through His audible voice speaking to us. In either of these instances, the Word that God speaks can be trusted and ministered with all full authority and assurance.

Dreams and Visions

Other common prophetic vehicles are dreams and visions. These are usually grouped together because each of these communicates God's words through images. There are believers that consistently have dreams and visions.

> *And it shall come to pass in the last days, saith God, I will pour out of my Spirit upon all flesh; and your sons and daughters shall prophesy, and your young men shall see VISIONS, and your old men shall DREAM*

dreams. (Joel 2:28 Emphasis mine)

Under the New Covenant, it is common for God to speak to believers in dreams and visions. Scripture shows us that God used dreams and visions to communicate with His people. Visions can be internal (in our spirits) and open (in clear view).

We also find in scripture there are certain individuals whom God chose to speak to regularly in dreams and in visions.

> *If there arise among you a prophet, or a DREAMER OF DREAMS, and giveth thee a sign or a wonder... (Deuteronomy 13:1 Emphasis mine)*

At times, the dreams and visions given need interpretation. It is within the interpretation that the word of prophecy is found. In addition, there are times that the dream and/or vision communicates God's prophetic word plainly. In this instance, no interpretation is needed. The dream has to be recalled as it was shown.

> *The prophet that hath a dream, let him tell a dream. (Jeremiah 23:28a)*

Prophetic Perception

Another common prophetic vehicle is that of prophetic perception. In this instance, the word of the Lord does not come to the believer, but the believer perceives and knows what God is saying. Paul alludes to this truth in his writings.

> *Now concerning virgins I have no commandment of the Lord: yet I give my judgment, as one that hath obtained mercy of the Lord to be faithful. (I Corinthians 7:25)*

Paul gave spiritual instruction to the Corinthians (in this instance) not because God spoke to him directly, but because he knew that what he said echoed the Lord's sentiments. Since the Holy Spirit dwells in the believer, there are times when we will know what the Lord is saying concerning ourselves, others, and occurrences without having any spiritual experience.

This phenomenon is the demonstration of what Paul taught when he said we have the mind of Christ.

> *But he that is spiritual judgeth all things, yet he himself is judged of no man. For who hath known the mind of the Lord, that he may instruct him? But we have the mind of Christ. (I Corinthians 2:15-16)*

We can judge all things; that is, perceive what God is saying and doing (prophetically) because the mind of Christ develops in us as we mature and grow in Him.

Prophetic Events

Another prophetic vehicle used by God to reveal His word to us is prophetic events. Common every day events sometimes will reveal the word of the Lord. The prophets oftentimes received what the Lord was saying through natural events.

This prophetic vehicle is oftentimes overlooked in the Body of Christ. Yet, if we are prayerful and watchful, God may be trying to communicate with us through events in our lives. Saul, Israel's first king, disobeyed God continually.

He refused to follow the Lord with his whole heart. Through Samuel, God instructed him to kill the whole nation of the Amalekites, including the livestock. However, he spared the king and some of the animals to sacrifice to God. After Samuel rebuked him for his disobedience, Saul begged him to return with him. As Samuel walked away from him, this happened.

> *And as Samuel turned about to go away, he laid hold upon the skirt of his mantle, and it rent. And Samuel said unto him, The Lord hath rent the kingdom of Israel from thee this day, and hath given it to a neighbour of thine, that is better than thou. And also the Strength of Israel will not lie nor repent: for he is not a man, that he should repent. (I Samuel 15:27-29)*

When Samuel's garment tore, God revealed to him a prophetic word for Saul. The same is demonstrated in the Church. Seemingly mundane and accidental events are used as vehicles for prophetic revelation.

Prayer

One of the safest prophetic vehicles is that of prayer. Believers are instructed to be consistent in prayer. However, there are believers who receive most of their prophetic revelation during prayer. Prayer is considered a safe prophetic vehicle because attention and focus is placed solely on the Lord.

In the scriptures, Daniel serves as an excellent example of God revealing prophetic information in prayer. He and the three Hebrew boys (men) prayed that Daniel would receive the interpretation of Nebuchadnezzar's dream.

> *Then Daniel went in, and desired of the king that he would give him time, and that he would shew the king the interpretation. Then Daniel went to his house, and made the thing*

known to Hananiah, Mishael, and Azariah, his companions: That they would desire mercies of the God of heaven concerning this secret; that Daniel and his fellows should not perish with the rest of the wise men of Babylon. (Daniel 2:16-18)

Daniel prayed that he would receive prophetic information. As he and the others prayed unto the Lord, prophetic understanding and revelation was given to Daniel. If you want to grow in the reception of prophetic revelation, increase your prayer life. You will discover that God is more than willing to reveal things to come.

Angels

Angels are sent by God to aid the believer. Both Testaments agree to the fact that God used angels to reveal prophetic information to His servants. In the Old Testament, we can look to Daniel again. After he prayed and petitioned the Lord, God sent an angel to reveal to him prophetic revelation.

> *And whiles I was speaking, and praying, and confessing my sin and the sin of my people Israel, and presenting my supplication before the Lord my God for the holy mountain of my God; Yea, whiles I was speaking in prayer, even the man Gabriel, whom I had seen in the vision at the beginning, being caused to fly swiftly, touched me about the time of the evening oblation. And he informed me, and talked with me, and said, O Daniel, I am now come forth to give thee skill and understanding. (Daniel 9:20-22)*

God used Gabriel in the New Testament to reveal to Mary of her purpose. While he communicated with her, he revealed prophetic information concerning her cousin.

> *And, behold, thy cousin Elisabeth, she hath also conceived a son in her old age: and this is the sixth month with her, who was called barren. (Luke 1:36)*

After the Church was established, God used angels. While Paul was traveling as a prisoner to Rome, an angel revealed to him what was going to happen.

> *For there stood by me this night the angel of God, whose I am, and whom I serve, Saying, Fear not, Paul; thou must be brought before Caesar: and, lo, God hath given thee all them that sail with thee. (Acts 27:23-24)*

Some believe this occurrence is rare, but God is the one who chooses how to deliver His word to His people for ministry.

The Scriptures

The safest prophetic vehicle is the word of God. Personal prophetic words that contain scriptures prove to be rich and powerful. The word of God is a more sure word of prophecy. It will not change or alter. We have called it prophecy from the sure prophecy.

> *We have also a more sure word of prophecy; whereunto ye do well that ye take heed, as unto a light that shineth in a dark place, until the day dawn and the daystar arise in your hearts. (2 Peter 1:19)*

God will bring to mind passages of scripture to be quoted to an individual. This type of prophecy will seldom come in error and at the wrong time. If you want a powerful and rich prophetic ministry, study the scriptures. It will prove to be the basis for a substantial prophetic gift.

Though there are numerous ways God can communicate to us, the seven prophetic vehicles mentioned are the most common. They will be useful guides in discerning prophetic operations.

3

The Prophetic Ministry

The word of prophecy comes to believers in different ways. Thus, the word of prophecy is administered in different ways. God uses individuals differently though they have the same office and gifts. Just as there are differences in the prophetic vehicle, there is diversity in prophetic ministry.

We stated in chapter 2 that Paul spoke of the diversity in the operation and function of the gifts in I Corinthians 12.

Now there are diversities of gifts, but the same Spirit. And there are differences of administrations, but the same Lord. And there are diversities of operations, but it is the same God which worketh all in all. But the manifestation of the Spirit is given to every man to profit withal. (I Corinthians 12:4-7)

An individual with any type of prophetic ministry will have to be sensitive to God's direction in delivering the word of the Lord. In this chapter, we will examine the different methods of prophetic ministry.

Those who are called to prophesy in any manner will develop certain patterns in how God uses them. Let us now explore the five most common demonstrations of prophetic ministry.

Spoken Word

The most widely seen demonstration of prophetic ministry is in the spoken word. When prophecy is given in this method, the one prophesying communicates word for word and verbatim what was said to them. The prophetic ministry comes as a result of direct revelation and inspiration.

The first aspect of prophetic ministry that is spoken occurs when the Lord speaks to a prophetic individual. Afterwards, they retell what the Lord said. This nature of prophetic ministry is what we call, prophetic parroting. The same way a parrot repeats what it hears, so does the believer in relation to God's words. In this instance, prophetic ministry is the result of revelation.

> *And Micaiah said, As the Lord liveth, what the Lord saith unto me, that will I speak. (I Kings 22:14)*

Micaiah would only speak what he heard the Lord say to him. The other aspect to prophetic ministry that is spoken is the inspirational. This nature of prophetic ministry is referred to as prophetic musing. The same way a writer, poet, or musician waits for inspiration before they can write or play, so does certain prophetic individuals.

> *Then upon Jahaziel the son Zechariah, the son of Benaiah, the son of Jeiel, the son of Mattaniah, a Levite of the sons of Asaph, came the Spirit of the Lord in the midst of the congregation; And he said, Hearken ye, all Judah, and ye inhabitants of Jerusalem, and thou king Jehoshaphat, Thus saith the Lord unto you... (2 Chronicles 20:14-15)*

There are times when they will prophesy based upon the inspiration of the moment. The Spirit of the Lord will come upon them. They will have no previous revelation of what to say. As they prophecy, the Lord brings to their heart, mind, and spirit what to say. This is a common way the word of prophecy is given.

Singing & Playing Music

Another way God inspires believers to minister His words is through song and music. This form of prophetic ministry is the same as the spoken word, except the prophetic word is sang and not spoken.

Paul spoke of this type of prophetic ministry as he explained tongues and the interpretation of tongues. We know that the interpretation of tongues is the same as prophecy.

I would that ye all spake with tongues; but rather that ye prophesied: for greater is he that prophesieth than he that speaketh with tongues, except he interpret, that the church may receive edifying. (I Corinthians 14:5)

After explaining the value of the interpretation of tongues, Paul spoke about singing in tongues and singing with the understanding or interpretation (which equals prophecy).

> *What is it then? I will pray with the spirit, and I will pray with the understanding also: I will sing with the spirit, and I will sing with the understanding also. (I Corinthians 14:15)*

In the book of Zephaniah, God states that He would joy over His people with singing. This shows that those who are prophetically gifted may sing God's words.

> *The Lord thy God in the midst of thee is mighty; he will save, he will rejoice over thee with joy; he will rest in his love, he will joy over thee with singing. (Zephaniah 3:17)*

Remember, much of David's psalms (which were

songs) were prophecies concerning the Messiah.

Some may ask, how can we prophesy on instruments? When David set up worship in Israel, he appointed musicians who were to prophesy on the instruments.

> *Moreover David and the captains of the host separated to the service of the sons of Asaph, and of Heman, and of Jeduthun, who should prophesy with harps, with psalteries, and with cymbals... (I Chronicles 25:1)*

Prophetic ministry in this form ministers unto the Lord by declaring His greatness. It also ministers God's love, grace, and peace to the hearers as the instruments are played under inspiration. Prophetic music brings God's refreshing, strength, healing, and encouragement through the melody made on the instruments.

Interpretation of Tongues

Prophetic ministry is demonstrated in the gift of interpretation of tongues. This form of prophetic ministry is unique in the fact that it is dependent upon the operation of another gift. The interpretation of tongues is the only gift that cannot stand alone.

One is able to prophesy, speak in tongues, speak a word of knowledge, heal, have faith, work miracles, discern spirits, and speak a word of wisdom, independently of the others. However, when it comes forth, it performs the same function as prophecy.

I would that ye all spake with tongues; but rather that ye prophesied: for greater is he that prophesieth than he that speaketh with tongues, except he interpret, that the church may receive edifying. (I Corinthians 14:5)

If any man speak in an unknown tongue, let it be by two, or at the most by three, and that by course; and let one interpret. (I Corinthians 14:27)

The interpretation of tongues provides exhortation, edification, and comfort to the Church. It can be spoken or sang. This form of prophetic ministry facilitates unity among believers since it does not stand alone.

A final thought: If you speak in unknown tongues, *pray for this gift.* Interpretation is **equal** to prophecy.

Wherefore let him that speaketh in an unknown tongue pray that he may interpret. (I Corinthians 14:13)

37

Prophetic Demonstration

In the Old Testament, a common way to administer the prophetic word was through demonstration then explanation. The prophet acted out the word of the Lord. As the people questioned their actions, they would explain what the acts meant.

Isaiah, Jeremiah, and Ezekiel will serve as brief examples of this type of prophetic ministry.

> *At the same time spake the Lord by Isaiah the son of Amoz, saying, Go and loose the sackcloth from off thy loins, and put off thy shoe from thy foot. And he did so, walking naked and barefoot. (Isaiah 20:2)*

Isaiah had to walk around partially nude to show the nation how they would be carried away into captivity.

> *In the beginning of the reign of Jehoiakim the son of Josiah king of Judah came this word unto Jeremiah from the Lord, saying ,Thus saith the Lord to me; Make thee bonds and yokes, and put them upon thy neck. (Jeremiah 27:1-2)*

Jeremiah had to walk around with a yoke on his neck to prophetically illustrate to the people how to submit to the invading Babylonians.

> *Therefore, thou son of man, prepare thee stuff for removing, and remove by day in their sight; and thou shalt remove from thy place to another place in their sight: it may be they will consider, though they be a rebellious house. (Ezekiel 12:3)*

Ezekiel, prophetically, demonstrated how the king

would try to escape going into captivity.

This form of prophetic ministry did not end with the deaths of the Old Testament prophets. In the book of Acts, we discover that the prophet Agabus used prophetic demonstration to deliver a prophecy.

> *And as we tarried there many days, there came down from Judaea a certain prophet, named Agabus. And when he was come unto us, he took Paul's girdle, and bound his own hands and feet, and said, Thus saith the Holy Ghost, So shall the Jews at Jerusalem bind the man that owneth this girdle, and shall deliver him into the hands of the Gentiles. (Acts 21:10-11)*

Agabus delivered the prophecy to Paul after he prophetically demonstrated what would befall him. This form of prophetic ministry gives the hearer visual stimulation along with the prophetic revelation.

Written Word

The final form of prophetic ministry to be discussed is that of the written word. This is the only type of prophetic ministry that needs no verbal assistance. There are times when God will instruct you to write someone what He is saying rather than deliver the prophecy orally. The reason for this is reserved for God alone. However, we cannot be afraid to follow the Lord in this manner.

Both Old and New Testament examples help to illustrate this type of prophetic ministry. In the Old Testament, Jeremiah and others were instructed to write their prophecies down. At times, prophecies to foreign nations were delivered in this manner.

The word that came to Jeremiah from the Lord, saying, Thus speaketh the Lord God of Israel, saying, Write thee all the words that I have spoken unto thee in a book. (Jeremiah 30:1-2)

In the New Testament, John was instructed to write down the prophecies given to him in the Book of Revelation.

Saying, I am Alpha and Omega, the first and the last: and, What thou seest, write in a book, and send it unto the seven churches which are in Asia; unto Ephesus, and unto Smyrna, and unto Pergamos, and unto Thyatira, and unto Sardis, and unto Philadelphia, and unto Laodicea. Revelation 1:11)

Write the things which thou hast seen, and the things which are, and the

*things which shall be hereafter.
(Revelation 1:19)*

This form of prophetic ministry is vital. When prophecies are delivered in written form, the person can continually be blessed every time it is read. It helps to serve as a reminder of what the Lord has said. Even if the Lord gives no command to write down the prophecy, it should be written and recorded when possible, for future use.

Though prophetic ministry manifests in various ways, the discussed five are the most prevalent in the Church.

4

The Prophetic Desire

Prophecy brings men and women into the heart and mind of God. Through this gift, God reveals His plan and purpose for our lives. Prophecy is a gift reserved for the benefit of believers.

Wherefore tongues are for a sign, not to them that believe, but to them that believe not: but prophesying serveth not for them that believe not, but for them which believe. (I Corinthians 14:22)

The prophetic spirit is one of the Lord's chief avenues of imparting knowledge of His wisdom and ways to the Church. When the gift of prophecy is in operation, the whole Church is built up in Christ. Since prophecy is important to the furtherance of the Church, Paul instructed the believers to desire this gift.

Desire to Prophesy

The church at Corinth had numerous problems. Among these was competition and confusion concerning the spiritual gifts. Individuals were dominating services with utterances in unknown tongues without any interpretation of these tongues. They were using the gift of tongues to appear spiritual.

Paul told them that if they spoke in unknown tongues without interpretation, the Church received no edification. He, then, encouraged the believers to covet the gifts that edified the Church; namely, prophecy.

Follow after charity, and desire spiritual gifts,

but rather that ye may prophesy. For he that speaketh in an unknown tongue speaketh not unto men, but unto God: for no man understandeth him; howbeit in the spirit he speaketh mysteries. But he that prophesieth speaketh unto men to edification, and exhortation, and comfort. He that speaketh in an unknown tongue edifieth himself; but he that prophesieth edifieth the church. (I Corinthians 14:1-4)

Some believers have misinterpreted God's command to covet the gift of prophecy. They covet the operation of the gift. They should rather covet the function of the gift. When you covet the operation of the gift, you are no better than the Corinthian believers. You only want to be seen and praised for your spirituality.

Even so ye, forasmuch as ye are zealous of spiritual gifts, seek that ye may excel to the edifying of the church. (I Corinthians 14:12)

When you covet the function of the gift, you want the Church to be edified through the prophetic ministry in you. Do not think that prophecy is reserved for special individuals. If your motives are right for asking for this gift, you can expect to receive it.

Desire to Love

If you want an effective and lasting prophetic gift, you have to walk in love. If love is not your motivation for using the prophetic gift, your ministry will be fruitless. After Paul encouraged the believers to covet the best gifts, he interjected that the gifts would mean nothing without love. This holds especially true for prophecy.

Consider Paul's words:

Though I speak with the tongues of men and of angels, and have not charity, I am become as sounding brass, or a tinkling cymbal. And though I have the gift of prophecy, and understand all mysteries, and all knowledge; and though I have all faith, so that I could remove mountains, and have not charity, I am nothing. And though I bestow all my goods to feed the poor, and though I give my body to be burned, and have not charity, it profiteth me nothing. Charity suffereth long, and is kind; charity envieth not; charity vaunteth not itself, is not puffed up, Doth not behave itself unseemly, seeketh not her own, is not easily provoked, thinketh no evil; Rejoiceth not in iniquity, but rejoiceth in the truth; Beareth all things, believeth all things, hopeth all things, endureth all things. Charity never faileth: but whether there be prophecies, they shall fail; whether there be tongues, they shall cease;

whether there be knowledge, it shall vanish away. (I Corinthians 13:1-8)

Rediscovering the Purpose

To strengthen our discussion on the gift of prophecy, we have developed an acronym, **P.R.O.P.H.E.C.Y.,** to help in our rediscovery of the purpose of prophecy, and what it performs. The purpose of the gift of prophecy is it:

P – Prepares us for what is next. Prophecy reveals to us what is God's purpose for our lives. It gives us insight into the path that is before us.

> *Behold, I will do a new thing; now it shall spring forth; shall ye not know it? I will even make a way in the wilderness, and rivers in the desert. (Isaiah 43:19)*

R – Reveals the mind of God. Prophecy brings us into a greater level of understanding who God is. The prophetic word reveals His character.

> *For who hath known the mind of the Lord, that he may instruct him? But we have the mind of Christ. (I Corinthians 2:16)*

O – Orders our steps. Prophecy provides direction for the hearer. God orders our steps through the prophetic word. We can receive clear direction of what we are to do next.

> *The steps of a good man are ordered by the Lord: and he delighteth in his way. (Psalm 37:23)*

P – Propels us into action. Prophecy motivates the hearer into action. There are times when believers become stagnant in their walks. The prophetic word provides the motivation needed for advancement.

The word which came to Jeremiah from the Lord, saying, Arise, and go down to the potter's house, and there I will cause thee to hear my words. (Jeremiah 18:1-2)

H – Helps our infirmities. Prophecy provides assistance to the believer in times of fear and weakness. Prophecy can reveal sources of spiritual warfare and reveal answers to troubling situations.

Likewise the Spirit also helpeth our infirmities... (Romans 8:26)

E – Elevates our minds. Prophecy produces in the hearer knowledge of spiritual things. The gift of prophecy not only reveals personal information, but spiritual information also.

For ye may all prophesy one by one, that all may LEARN, and all may be comforted.(I Corinthians 14:31, Emphasis mine)

C – Challenges us in our relationship with the Lord. Prophecy comes to correct ungodly behavior and influences. It comes, at times, to provide discipline for the hearer.

> *For whom the Lord loveth he chasteneth, and scourgeth every son whom he receiveth. If ye endure chastening, God dealeth with you as with sons; for what son is he whom the father chasteneth not? (Hebrews 12:6-7)*

Y – Yields results in spiritual growth. Prophecy inspires spiritual growth in the recipients. Prophecy will cause fruitfulness in the spiritual life of the believer.

> *Herein is my Father glorified, that ye bear much fruit; so shall ye be my*

disciples. (John 15:8)

The gift of prophecy comes to reveal the plan of God, not the greatness of the one that is gifted. If we are humble in the administration of this gift, we will have fruitful ministries. Regardless of the magnitude of the prophetic gift, in God's eyes it accounts for nothing without love.

Love is the complete manifestation of any gift.

If you desire to prophesy, first ask the Lord for a greater level of love for the Body of Christ. In doing so, you will avoid the pitfalls of prophetic ministry.

In the following chapters, we will explore in detail how to avoid potential pitfalls in the execution and reception of prophetic ministry.

5

The Prophetic Problem

The gift of prophecy comes to edify. It comes to bring understanding and strength to the recipient. Yet, not all "prophetic" ministry produces these things. It has developed into a prophetic problem.

Problems in the operation of the gift of prophecy occur because of the vessel and not the gift.

But we have this treasure in earthen vessels, that the excellency of the power may be of God, and not of us. (2 Corinthians 4:10)

The believer is referred to as an earthen vessel. It was simply a pot made out of clay. However, if there is any crack, chip, or imperfection

55

on the inside of the pot, it could taint the contents. This is what happens in prophetic ministry. The treasure of the Holy Spirit is within us. But, if our vessels are not consistently cleansed and cared for, the ministry of the Spirit will be tainted by our thoughts, feelings, emotions, and ambitions.

In this chapter, we want to discuss the prophetic problem. The prophetic problem is that our personal feelings and ambitions taint the word that the Lord will speak through us. Within prophetic ministry, there are five levels of ministry.

Regardless of your place in the prophetic (gift of prophecy, prophetic anointing, or the office of the prophet), knowledge of these levels is important. Each one reflects the purity of the prophetic word given.

On the next page, we have placed a diagram showing the levels of prophetic ministry.

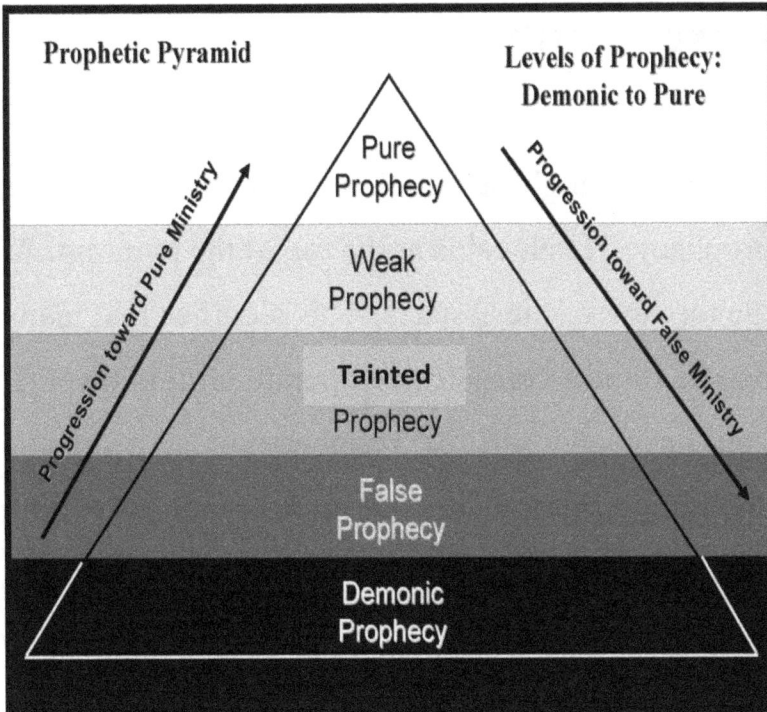

Prophetic Pyramid

Levels of Prophecy:
Demonic to Pure

Progression toward Pure Ministry

Progression toward False Ministry

Pure
Prophecy

Weak
Prophecy

Tainted
Prophecy

False
Prophecy

Demonic
Prophecy

The highest level of prophetic ministry is pure prophecy and the lowest level is demonic prophecy. Because of this range, mishaps in the prophetic are likely to happen.

As we examine each level in the prophetic, discover your own vulnerabilities in order to excel operating in a pure prophetic gift.

Pure Prophecy

The highest level of prophecy is pure prophecy. This level is at the top of the pyramid. At the top, there is less space. This signifies that many people do not consistently operate on this level. If you have the gift of prophecy or a prophetic anointing, every effort has to be made to remain pure in ministry.

> *Because strait is the gate, and narrow is the way, which leadeth unto life, and few there be that find it. (Matthew 7:14)*

Jesus said concerning eternal life that there are few that find it. The same is true for pure prophetic ministry. There are few in the Body that consistently minister purely in the prophetic.

To operate in pure prophecy, the person

must deliver what God said and, in the manner, that it was said. The mind and heart of God has to be communicated.

> *And he said unto me, Son of man, go, get thee unto the house of Israel, and speak with my words unto them. (Ezekiel 3:4)*

Pure prophecy contains God's words only. Though God uses us, we have to follow Him. To remain pure in the prophetic, one has to D.I.E to self.

D – Deny the impulse to impress others in ministry. Pride will cause individuals to add words and thoughts to what the Lord has said. Ministry should not be used to boost self-esteem.

> *Then said Jesus unto his disciples, If any man will come after me, let him deny himself, and take up his cross, and follow*

me. (Matthew 16:24)

I – Ignore the pressures of others. Those who are prophets and others who have the gift of prophecy sometimes are pressured to give prophecies. If they do not learn to ignore the pressure, they could operate in a soulish realm in ministry.

> *For do I now persuade men, or God? or do I seek to please men? for if I yet pleased men, I should not be the servant of Christ. (Galatians 1:10)*

E – Examine motives in ministry. If the individual does not minister for the right reasons, he/she will begin to operate in a tainted prophetic ministry. The only true motive is love.

> *Examine yourselves, whether ye be in the faith; prove your own selves. (2 Cor. 13:5)*

Weak Prophecy

The next level of prophecy is what we have termed weak prophecy. It is our belief that a significant portion of purported prophetic ministry is on this level. Weak prophecy is prophecy that lacks clarity, depth, and power.

Weak prophecies usually come across as words of exhortation and encouragement rather than the voice of the Lord.

Weak prophecy usually frustrates the hearer because it provides no revelation or significant direction from the Lord. Rather than edifying the listener, frustration occurs.

> *For if the trumpet give an uncertain sound, who shall prepare himself to the battle? (I Corinthians 14:8)*

Weak prophecy is like tongues without an interpretation. The source is God, but its effects are minimal. Weak prophecy comes when an individual hears from the Lord but does not wait or seek clarity for the initial revelation.

Weak prophecy sounds like this, "God says He is going to bless you," or "the Lord says He is going to work some things out for you." These words should encourage. However, what if I have numerous situations for which I am needing the Lord's intervention? The word does not bless me the way it should because I do not know what situation to apply it to.

To avoid operating in weak prophecy, one must **W.A.I.T.** on the Lord.

W – Wait on the Lord for further revelation before speaking. Patience is needed when listening.

For who hath stood in the counsel of the Lord, and hath perceived and heard his word? Who hath marked his word, and heard it? (Jeremiah 23:18)

A – Ask the Lord for clarity. This should be done in prayer. In the scriptures, the one receiving the word of the Lord sometimes entered into a dialogue with God for clearer focus.

For every one that asketh receiveth; and he that seeketh findeth; and to him that knocketh it shall be opened. (Matthew 7:8)

I – Ignore initial excitement and feelings when God speaks to you. When the prophetic word comes, it usually grabs hold of our natural senses. We feel God's power upon us which causes us to feel we have to speak immediately. This is not always the case. The Spirit may want to give more information to the hearer.

In whom are hid all the treasures of wisdom and knowledge. (Colossians 2:3)

T – Take Time to discern the Lord's timing. Another aspect that causes weak prophecy is speaking the prophecy too early or too late.

The Lord God hath given me the tongue of the learned, that I should know how to speak a word in season to him that is weary: he wakeneth morning by morning, he wakeneth mine ear to hear as the learned. (Isaiah 50:4)

Tainted Prophecy

The next lowest level of prophecy is what we have termed Tainted prophecy. This type of prophecy is a mixture of flesh and Spirit. It is mixed prophecy. The initial revelation is good, but then the one who is prophesying adds their own thoughts, opinions, and feelings concerning the revelation.

At other times, the one prophesying will add other information based upon a positive reception of their prophecy. They add more information to seem spiritual. This type of prophecy manifests in this manner: "God says He is going to bless you on your job." This part of the prophecy is God. However, the individual then adds, "You are going to get a promotion," or they say "It is going to happen in seven days." The last two statements came because the prophet of the moment added his/her thoughts, desiring to be spiritual.

Many in the Church have experienced this. Someone gives you a prophecy and you know that it is God. But, as they continue to talk red flags come up and you wonder about what was said. Usually in these cases, the person has operated in tainted prophecy. To deal with this type of prophecy, discernment and forgiveness is needed. Discernment is needed to keep the part of the prophecy that is good.

> *Despise not prophesyings. Prove all things; hold fast that which is good. (I Thessalonians 5:20-21)*

Forgiveness is needed so that you will not defame, mistrust, or become angry with the one who gave the word. In these situations, prayer and humility will help because God may send this person to you again and the prophecy may be pure.

To avoid operating in this level of prophecy, one has to **W.A.S.H.**

W – Be Watchful. One has to be mindful of their own thoughts. The one with the prophetic gift has to recognize the difference between their voice and the Lord's. If one does not watch, he will be tempted to add invalid information.

> *Watch and pray, that ye enter not into temptation: the spirit indeed is willing, but the flesh is weak. (Matthew 26:41)*

A – Acknowledge error. The one prophesying has to be willing to admit when they have missed the mark or operated in a mixture. This sets them up for forgiveness and future acceptance. In addition, the Lord will give them the grace they need to operate in a pure prophetic flow.

> *But he giveth more grace. Wherefore he saith, God resisteth the proud, but giveth grace unto the humble. (James 4:6)*

S – Say only what is received. The individual has to learn to only say what the Lord gives them prophetically. Discipline is needed in this area. In doing so, the individual will not operate in this realm.

> *Thus shall ye say everyone to his neighbour,
> and every one to his brother, What hath the
> Lord answered? and, What hath the Lord
> spoken? (Jeremiah 23:35)*

H – Hush. The one prophesying has to stop
talking when God stops. This is where many
individuals fall. God will speak to them
accurately, but because they are feeling good and
the anointing is still upon them, they will
continue to prophesy after the Spirit stopped
speaking.

God gave a grave warning to individuals
who would try to add to the prophecies given in
the Book of Revelation. This should help us walk
in fear in prophetic ministry.

> *For I testify unto every man that heareth the*

words of the prophecy of this book, If any man shall add unto these things, God shall add unto him the plagues that are written in this book. (Revelation 22:18)

False Prophecy

False prophecy is prophecy whose source is not from the Lord. It is understood that false prophecy normally comes from false ministers and false saints. However, there are saints of God who operate in false prophecy. False prophecy comes when individuals speak for God without the Lord saying anything.

Son of man, prophesy against the prophets of Israel that prophesy, and say thou unto them that prophesy out of their own hearts, Hear ye the word of the Lord; Thus saith the Lord

God; Woe unto the foolish prophets, that follow their own spirit, and have seen nothing! (Ezekiel 13:2-3)

I want to interject a note here. A false prophet is not only someone who is an ungodly person. A believer can be a false prophet FOR THE MOMENT when they misrepresent God in prophetic ministry. This occurs, at times, when believers are experiencing extremely difficult situations. They come to someone who has a prophetic gift.

The gifted individual feels compassion and gives a 'prophetic word' to calm the individual. The word came from their will and not God's mouth. This occurs frequently. The individual is not a false Christian, but the prophecy is.

False prophecy also manifests when individuals use expressions like, "Let me speak a word in your life," or "You can prophesy to yourself or your situation," and the like. If the source of prophecy is supposed to be God, we cannot prophesy at will. It has to be done in accordance to what God is saying.

We sometimes confuse prophecy with faith declarations. When this is done, false prophecy occurs. To escape operating in false prophecy, one has to **P.R.A.Y.**

P – Pray consistently. To avoid false prophecy, the believer has to have a prayer life. In doing so, he will be sensitive to the voice of God. He will know when God is speaking and when He is not. This will ensure that they will not speak until He does.

> *But ye, beloved, building up yourselves on your most holy faith, praying in the Holy Ghost. (Jude 1:20)*

R – Reverence God. If the believer fears the Lord, he will not be presumptuous in ministering in His name. Remember, those who minister (in any form) will receive a greater judgment from the Lord.

> *My brethren, be not many masters, knowing that we shall receive the greater condemnation. (James 3:1)*

A – Acknowledge no revelation. Believers have to acknowledge to themselves and others when God is not speaking. Some feel that if they say they do not have a word, people will lose respect for them. In turn, they give false prophecies to retain face. This is a trap and snare of the enemy.

> *And the man of God said, Let her alone; for her soul is vexed within her: and the Lord hath hid it from me, and hath not told me. (2 Kings 4:27b)*

Y – Yield to caution. The yield sign in traffic means to proceed with caution. To avoid false prophecy, individuals have to move in ministry with caution and discretion. This helps to overcome error.

> *See then that ye walk circumspectly, not as fools, but as wise. (Ephesians 5:15)*

Demonic Prophecy

The lowest form of prophetic ministry is demonic prophecy. This is prophetic ministry through demonic influence. Again, we know that those who are false prophets, psychics, soothsayers, diviners, and the like operate in this realm of prophecy. However, there are believers who have treaded in this area.

Demonic prophecy can sometimes be hard

to recognize because it will contain valid information. The woman who followed Paul and his company had the right information, but from the wrong source.

> *And it came to pass, as we went to prayer, a certain damsel possessed with a spirit of divination met us, which brought her masters much gain by soothsaying: The same followed Paul and us, and cried, saying, These men are the servants of the most high God, which shew unto us the way of salvation. (Acts 16:16-17)*

Though believers are to be filled with the Spirit, some open themselves up to operate in demonic prophetic ministry. How does this happen?

There are three main factors:

1. It occurs in believers who do not have the gift of

prophecy or a prophetic anointing but try to prophesy anyway. They open themselves up to receive "revelation" regardless of the source. Because some information is true, they may feel that God is speaking to them when He is not.

> *For as we have many members in one body, and all members have not the same office. (Romans 12:4)*

2. It occurs in believers who have valid prophetic gifts but operate beyond their measure of anointing and gifting. They begin to think anything they say is prophetic or from the Lord. When this happens, they leave a door open for the adversary to use them.

> *Having then gifts differing according to the grace that is given to us, whether prophecy, let us prophesy according to the proportion of faith. (Romans 12:6)*

3. It occurs in believers who prophesy with unforgiveness and hurt in their lives. They are bitter individuals. These individuals will prophesy to get back at others and vent. If this is done consistently, the enemy will take opportunity to infuse his words into their prophecies.

> *Repent therefore of this thy wickedness, and pray God, if perhaps the thought of thine heart may be forgiven thee. For I perceive that thou art in the gall of bitterness, and in the bond of iniquity. (Acts 8:22-23)*

Another aspect of demonic prophecy is that it brings the listeners into bondage. Prophecies that create fear, cause tension, negative divisions, illnesses, and the like are demonically induced.

Prophecy does challenge believers, but it will convict, heal, discipline, correct, and exhort individuals without breaking their resolve to serve the Lord. To avoid this type of ministry or be delivered from it, one has to F.A.S.T.

F – Forsake the desire for notoriety. One of the major factors in demonic prophecy is that the individual wants to be special. The gift of prophecy, to them, will make them special. The only way to close this door is to seek servant hood and not salutations.

But he that is greatest among you shall be your servant. (Matthew 23:11)

A – Acknowledge the lack of true prophetic gifting. Others flow in demonic prophecy because they want a gift they do not possess. If they are a believer, in their inner man, they know this. If they humble themselves and admit to no gifting, cleansing and deliverance will take place.

For as we have many members in one

body, and all members have not the same office. (Romans 12:4)

S – Seek the will of God. Believers who fall into this realm do not have a solid sense of their identity in Christ. Others are not satisfied with what God gave them to do.

A return to God's will has to be done to avoid and overcome operating in this lowest form of prophecy.

Then said I, Lo, I come (in the volume of the book it is written of me,) to do thy will, O God. (Hebrews 10:7)

T – Take authority over your spirit. Those who have been involved in this realm of prophetic ministry have no control over their spiritual experiences. They claim that God is so "heavy" upon them and they have to speak. However, the scriptures declare otherwise.

One must be mindful of what force is trying to have influence in his/her spirit. In doing so, demonic prophecy will not be a part of ministry.

If anything be revealed to another that sitteth by, let the first hold his peace. For ye may all prophesy one by one, that all may learn, and all may be comforted. And the spirits of the prophets are subject to the prophets. (I Corinthians 14:30-32)

The Prophetic Problem is something the Church will combat until Christ's return. However, if members in the Body will recognize their vulnerabilities in these areas, a pure prophetic flow will make it easier to handle. The aforementioned warnings and explanations are guidelines to recognizing counterfeit and tainted prophetic ministry and not the rule. The revelation of the

Spirit is to be sought in all situations regarding the word of prophecy. If we can overcome the negative aspects of prophetic ministry, the misery that occurs because of these mishaps will be minimal.

6

The Prophetic Confusion

The gift of prophecy is unique. Unlike the other gifts, the gift of prophecy has a personal tone in its operation. In both Testaments, the individuals who prophesied prefaced their statements with "Thus says the Lord," or "The Lord says." These statements reflect the personal involvement of God in man's affairs. However, other gifts of the Spirit have been called prophecy when they are not.

In the previous chapter, we examined the mishaps in the prophetic caused by bad prophetic ministry. Now, we will diffuse the prophetic confusion. We will examine the gift of prophecy versus the other revelatory gifts.

For to one is given by the Spirit the word of

wisdom; to another the word of knowledge by the same Spirit. To another the working of miracles; to another prophecy; to another discerning of spirits; to another divers kinds of tongues; to another the interpretation of tongues. (I Corinthians 12:8, 10)

It is commonplace today for a believer to walk up to a brother or sister and say, "I have a word for you." Oftentimes, the individual saying it has no clue what that means. As soon as we hear this expression, we think that a word of prophecy is to follow.

How many of us have been disappointed when it was something we already knew, or they only told us something that we should do? This was because they did not realize they had no word of prophecy, but only a word of knowledge or a word of wisdom.

The gift of prophecy is often confused with the operation of the revelation gifts. They are the word of knowledge, the word of wisdom, and the discerning of spirits. As we examine each of these gifts, we will explain each gift, how each differs from the gift of prophecy, and how each works alongside the gift of prophecy.

Prophecy vs. the Word of Knowledge

The word of knowledge is a gift where the Spirit of God reveals facts about individuals and situations from the mind of God. I believe we all have experienced this gift in one form or another.

Many times, when you know something is going to happen or when you just "know" something about an individual or situation without any outside influence; it is usually a manifestation of this gift.

When we consider the gifts of the Spirit, we feel that when God reveals something, it should be extraordinary. However, we have numerous examples in scripture where God would reveal common things to His people. Therefore, when this gift manifests today outside of a ministry setting, believers overlook it occasionally. Facts revealed through the word of knowledge may deal with things in the past and present. Let us now examine the operation of this gift in scripture.

> *At that time Abijah the son of Jeroboam fell sick. And Jeroboam said to his wife, Arise, I pray thee, and disguise thyself, that thou be not known to be the wife of Jeroboam; and get thee to Shiloh: behold, there is Ahijah the prophet, which told me that I should be king over this people. And take with thee ten loaves, and cracknels, and a cruse of honey, and go to him: he shall tell thee what shall become of the child. And Jeroboam's wife did*

so, and arose, and went to Shiloh, and came to the house of Ahijah. But Ahijah could not see; for his eyes were set by reason of his age. And the Lord said unto Ahijah, Behold, the wife of Jeroboam cometh to ask a thing of thee for her son; for he is sick: thus and thus shalt thou say unto her: for it shall be, when she cometh in, that she shall feign herself to be another woman. (I Kings 14:1-5)

Even though Ahijah was a prophet, God spoke to him through the word of knowledge. God revealed facts to him about the situation. He told him that Jeroboam's son was sick, his wife was coming, and she was pretending to be another woman. Today, if someone has this type of information concerning a situation, we call it prophecy. Again, the word of knowledge is just what it says – knowledge concerning certain individuals and situations.

The word of knowledge differs from prophecy in two ways. First, the word of knowledge only gives us information concerning a circumstance or situation. However, the gift of prophecy introduces us to God's perspective on the facts in the circumstance or situation. Much of the weak prophecy in the Church is usually a manifestation of the word of knowledge masking as prophecy. The word of knowledge normally comes as the set-up for the gift of prophecy to operate.

Prophecy vs. the Word of Wisdom

The word of wisdom is very similar to the word of knowledge, but its function is broader. The word of wisdom gives us insight into the plan of God and shows us how to apply the word of knowledge or prophecy. It does what it says; it brings God's wisdom into an individual's life or situation. It also brings us into God's eternal purpose. Consider Christ's words,

> *Therefore also said the wisdom of God, I will send them prophets and apostles, and some of them they shall slay and persecute. (Luke 11:49)*

Jesus spoke of God's plan through the word of wisdom. The word of wisdom oftentimes speaks of future events in the mind of God. The word of wisdom sometimes appears in the form of a warning, telling us what we should or should not do. The scriptures give an excellent example of this:

> *Now when much time was spent, and when sailing was now dangerous, because the fast was now already past, Paul admonished them, And said unto them, Sirs, I perceive that this voyage will be with hurt and much damage, not only of the lading and ship, but also of our lives. Then fearing lest we should*

have fallen upon rocks, they cast four anchors out of the stern, and wished for the day. And as the shipmen were about to flee out of the ship, when they had let down the boat into the sea, under colour as though they would have cast anchors out of the foreship, Paul said to the centurion and to the soldiers, Except these abide in the ship, ye cannot be saved. (Acts 27:9-10, 29-31)

This is a familiar story to us all. Twice, Paul spoke up with the word of wisdom to save his life and those that were on the ship. The word of wisdom came and he told them the voyage would be deadly. Consequently, they ignored him.

After the storm arose and they were in trouble, the word of wisdom came forth again. He told them that except everyone stays on the ship, they could not be saved. They did not ignore him on this occasion; subsequently, everyone survived.

Sometimes we ignore the word of wisdom because it seems more like advice rather than revelation. We must have an ear to hear the instruction of the Spirit of God. It may mean the difference between life and death.

The word of wisdom is confused with prophecy because it will speak of future events. Prophecy usually contains the word of wisdom. It is God speaking to us and telling us what will happen. However, the revelation of the word of wisdom has no personal tone to it.

When Jesus spoke of God's word of wisdom, there was no single person identified, but the Jews as a nation. The word of wisdom will only draw you into understanding of God's plan, but not necessarily His heart for your situation.

Prophecy vs. the Discerning of Spirits

This gift has to be one of the most misunderstood gifts of those listed in I Corinthians 12. To understand the true essence of this gift, we must first understand what it means to discern. Discern means to differentiate, distinguish, observe, notice, perceive, and note. This shows us that this gift helps the believer to recognize the difference between spirits. It allows believers to know what spirit is behind any given activity.

> *Beloved, do not believe every spirit, but test the spirits to see whether they are from God, for many false prophets have gone out into the world. (I John 4:1 NASV)*

Because the Spirit of God dwells in the believer, each believer has the ability to discern to some degree. Yet, the individual that possesses this gift discerns with a greater level of clarity and accuracy. They can see into the realm of the spirit and identify what spirit is in operation; whether it is the spirit of man, the Spirit of God, or the spirit of the devil.

Even during the days of the apostles, discernment was very much needed. From the scriptures, we find an example of the operation of this gift.

> *And when Simon saw that through laying on of the apostles' hands the Holy Ghost was given, he offered them money, Saying, Give me also this power, that on whomsoever I lay hands, he may receive the Holy Ghost. But Peter said unto him, Thy money perish with thee, because thou hast thought that the gift of God may be purchased with money. Thou hast neither part nor lot in this matter: for thy heart is not right in the sight of God. Repent*

therefore of this thy wickedness, and pray God, if perhaps the thought of thine heart may be forgiven thee. For I perceive that thou art in the gall of bitterness, and in the bond of iniquity. (Acts 8:18-23)

Peter, through the discerning of spirits, perceived that Simon had made his request because his heart was not right. Peter discerned that bitterness was the poison of Simon's spirit and that iniquity had him in bondage. Peter could only make such a statement because he had discerned the spirit behind Simon's action.

Those who possess this gift must be careful not to become critical of others or become consumed with finding demonic activity. The purpose of this gift is not only for protection, but also to help us recognize God's working so that we can follow Him without fear.

The discerning of spirits is confused with prophecy because those who possess the prophetic gift are oftentimes seers. They see into the spirit. When someone says that they discern a particular spirit or force, some call it prophecy when they see the spirit or force manifest. They will say, "They prophesied and said this person had a spirit," or "They said this spirit would show up." This revelation did not come because of prophecy, but because they saw in the Spirit through this gift.

Prophecy and the Revelatory Gift

Once the prophetic confusion is overcome, we can fully appreciate how prophecy operates alongside the other gifts. We stated earlier that the word of knowledge usually paves the way for the gift of prophecy.

God will give an individual a word of

knowledge in order to get the hearer's attention. This is to give confidence to the hearer that the forthcoming prophecy can be trusted as from the Lord. In addition, the prophetic word may contain the word of knowledge to show individuals that God knows them personally.

Usually, the prophetic word will contain the word of wisdom. The word of wisdom enhances the prophetic word. When these two gifts are combined, the hearer understands the eternal presence of God. He is revealed as God, who is in control of all time.

Another way that prophecy works with the word of wisdom is that the word of wisdom gives us understanding of how to apply the prophetic word. At other instances, a word of wisdom will follow the prophecy to further clarify what was said.

The discerning of spirits functions like the word of knowledge in relation to prophecy. An individual is allowed to see by the Spirit and the word of prophecy comes to bring God's perspective on what is seen.

Prophecy is designed to work in harmony with the other gifts, and not to be confused with them. If this is understood, the gift of prophecy and prophetic ministry will be powerfully demonstrated. In addition, pitfalls will be avoided.

7

The Prophetic Perspective

There is much to consider in the delivery and reception of prophetic ministry. Thus, a proper perspective of prophetic ministry must be developed. Without a proper prophetic perspective, individuals will begin to despise prophecy because of the errors of others.

> *Quench not the Spirit. Despise not prophesyings. Prove all things; hold fast that which is good. (I Thessalonians 5:19-21)*

When we distrust prophetic ministry, it results in a quenching of the Spirit. God delights in revealing His mind to us through the prophetic Spirit.

But as it is written, Eye hath not seen, nor ear heard, neither have entered into the heart of

man, the things which God hath prepared for them that love him. But God hath revealed them unto us by his Spirit: for the Spirit searcheth all things, yea, the deep things of God. (I Corinthians 2:9-10)

In addition to despising prophecy, there are others who are afraid to trust prophecy. They fear that they will be misled. To walk in distrust and fear with regard to the prophetic ministry is not the will of God for the believer.

In this chapter, we will discuss how to avoid major pitfalls in prophetic ministry; namely, in Receiving Prophetic Ministry, Judging Prophetic Ministry, and Applying Prophetic Ministry.

As these areas of concern in the prophetic

are considered, the believer should be able to handle prophetic ministry (bad or good) properly.

Guidelines for Receiving Prophecy

To minimize the misery that comes from the mishaps of prophetic ministry, there are guidelines that believers can incorporate in the reception of prophetic ministry.

1) Be prayerful as the prophecy is given. While the individual is giving the prophetic word, pray silently in your spirit for clarity and understanding. This will help in recognizing the source of the prophetic word.

Pray without ceasing. (I Thess. 5:17)

2) Listen intently as the word of prophecy comes. Though true prophetic words come with the power and presence of the Spirit of the Lord, try earnestly to listen to the words that are spoken (especially if the prophecy is not being recorded). Sometimes the excitement of receiving a true word overcomes us. This will help in recognizing the intent of the word.

> *Give ye ear, and hear my voice; hearken, and hear my speech. (Isaiah 28:23)*

3) Receive the prophecy in a humble manner. There are times when a person's demeanor or manner will cause us to be hard or stubborn   when the word is given. Sometimes, we can miss what the Lord is saying because of this.

Even in cases when a prophetic word is impure or bogus, we are to handle them with grace and discretion.

> *Likewise, ye younger, submit yourselves unto the elder. Yea, all of you be subject one to*

another, and be clothed with humility: for God resisteth the proud, and giveth grace to the humble. (I Peter 5:5)

4) Consider the individual giving the word of prophecy. There are believers who may give you a bogus prophetic word, unintentionally. Remember to have compassion on the individual. Some will deliver the wrong prophetic word with good intentions. Do not use this time as an excuse to embarrass the individual.

After the time of ministry is over (if possible), talk to the one who gave the erroneous word in private. They may have a valid gift but moved in error for that moment. If this is not possible, remember to pray for the individual rather than tear down. You have to treat them like you would want to be treated, if you erred in ministry.

Brethren, if a man be overtaken in a fault, ye

which are spiritual, restore such an one in the spirit of meekness; considering thyself, lest thou also be tempted. (Galatians 6:1)

5) *If the word of prophecy given is true,* express this to the one who gave the word whenever possible. True prophetic gifts are under attack. The person prophesying can be strengthened and encouraged to go further in ministry based upon your positive response to their ministry. In this manner, the one prophesying also receives ministry.

And we beseech you, brethren, to know them which labour among you, and are over you in the Lord, and admonish you; And to esteem them very highly in love for their work's sake. And be at peace among yourselves. (I Thessalonians 5:12-13)

If the above guidelines are followed, prophetic ministry (good or bad) can be handled with courtesy and minimize damage in the lives of believers.

Guidelines for Judging Prophecy

One of the major facets of understanding prophecy is to discern when something is not prophecy. Judging prophecy can be a tough task at times. Nevertheless, the scriptures do give guidelines to us to help us as we strive to hear from God through others. We all want to receive from God, but some of us have lost faith in the gift of prophecy.

Many have received erroneous prophecies. Others have followed the directions given to them through prophecy and the results were unfavorable. When judging a prophetic word, we must be careful not to miss God.

Conversely, we need to know when God has

not spoken. If you are unsure as to how to hear from God through others, there are certain questions you can ask yourself. We must understand that God does speak to His people through this gift. We do not need to be afraid, but discerning. Even if we have received bad prophetic words in the past, we should not allow the enemy to steal a blessing from us. God may send someone with a valid prophetic word.

Does it come to pass? Sometimes this aspect of judging is hard to determine. However, if the person prophesying (prophet or laymen) gives a specific period or date for the word of the Lord to happen, it is easier to determine.

> *When a prophet speaketh in the name of the Lord, if the thing follow not, nor come to pass, that is the thing which the Lord hath not spoken, but the prophet hath spoken it presumptuously: thou shalt not be afraid*

of him. (Deuteronomy 18:22)

Conversely, do not be quick to brand the prophecy false because it did not occur when you expected it. Prayerfully consider the word. It may turn out to be valid, but you did not understand the time in which it was to happen.

Is it clear and understandable? Though God speaks to us in strange ways at times, the word of the Lord should be understandable; else, you will not know what to do. You cannot obey God if the word is unclear.

For God is not the author of confusion, but of peace, as in all the churches of the saints. (I Corinthians 14:33)

On the other hand, if you do not understand the word, ask the person who delivered the word for clarity. You may find that their choice of words was not clear rather than the prophecy being bogus. There may be times when the person prophesying may not know or remember what was said. However, it is our belief that if the word is from God, they should be able to explain more clearly what they received.

Does it agree with the Word? Prophecy will never instruct you to do something against the written word of God. The scriptures represent the purest expression of prophecy.

We have also a more sure word of prophecy; whereunto ye do well that ye take heed, as unto a light that shineth in a dark place, until the day of dawn, and the day star arise in our hearts. Knowing this first that no prophecy of scripture is of any private interpretation. For the prophecy came not in old time by the will of man: but holy men of God spake as they were moved by the Holy

Ghost. (2 Peter 1: 19-21)

Be humble in this area. Not every prophetic word has a direct correlation to the scripture. This is true for prophetic words that may deal with specific situations in your life. Be sure that the word given does not tell you to do anything against the Word.

Is it demonic, fleshly, or the Spirit of God? You must learn to recognize the source of the word. Is it in agreement with the will of God for your life?

> *Beloved, believe not every spirit, but test the spirits whether they are of God… (I John 4:1a)*

Please be wise in this area also. Sometimes, our own personal perceptions may hinder us from receiving from God. If we do not agree with a person's demeanor, we may say it was flesh. Remember, God uses people. Their attributes and personality traits may surface as the Spirit moves through them. Let not your own biases block you from hearing from God.

Does it agree with previous prophetic revelation? Sometimes individuals may prophesy their own will for your life. They will say things that you have never heard concerning you or your life in God. They may try to state prophetically that you are called to a ministry, or that you are supposed to take some sort of new direction in your life.

When this happens, judge the word according to previous prophetic utterances from the Lord.

> *This command I entrust to you, Timothy, my son, in accordance with the prophecies previously made concerning you... (I Timothy 1:18a, NASB)*

However, just because someone tells you something that God may not have previously revealed to you does not mean it is not from the Lord. Our walks with the Lord are progressive and so is His revelation concerning our lives.

Sometimes God will reveal something "new" to us in order to guide us into the next phase of our relationship with Him. Be prayerful when new prophetic revelation is given to you. It may very well be the voice of the Lord. The aforementioned guidelines are to help us in our efforts to receive from God. They are not to be used as excuses to reject the word of the Lord.

Sometimes, there will be prophetic words given to which the guidelines may tell you to reject it, but you may discover that the word is from God. Be humble and prayerful while you are trying to judge the prophetic word.

Guidelines for Applying Prophecy

Once a prophetic word is judged to be from the Lord, there are guidelines to applying or handling it. There are many who receive prophecies, but never see their fulfillment due to misappropriating the prophetic word. In order to see the fullness of the word of prophecy, proper application must be done.

1. Rehearse the prophecy in prayer. While in prayer, it is important to discuss the prophecy with the Lord. He may want to give you more information concerning the prophetic word. The scriptures declare that prophecy comes in part. Praying about the prophecy opens you up to further clarification and information.

For we know in part, and we prophesy in part. (I Corinthians 13:9)

2. Discuss the prophecy with mature believers.

Certain believers (leaders and prayer partners) may be able to help you understand other aspects of the prophecy. Sometimes we receive the prophecy in a biased manner. Other eyes may be able to see more clearly what the Lord is referring to with particular prophecies.

> *Where no counsel is, the people fall: but in the multitude of counselors there is safety. (Proverbs 11:14)*

3. Fulfill all known requirements for the prophecy's fulfillment.

Certain prophecies come with conditions of fulfillment. While you are waiting for God to do His work, do your part. In addition, some prophecies may not specifically outline conditions, but the conditions may be implied.

Regardless of the prophecy given, always remain in a strong relationship with the Lord. This will guarantee fulfillment.

> *And it shall come to pass, if thou shalt hearken diligently unto the voice of the Lord thy God... (Deuteronomy 28:1)*

4. Walk in faith until you see its fulfillment. The enemy will come to try to strip the believer of faith in the prophetic word. Therefore, fight the deception of the enemy with faith and the words of the prophecy.

> *That ye be not slothful, but followers of them who through faith and patience inherit the promises. (Hebrews 6:12)*

Handling and receiving prophetic ministry can be difficult at times. However, if practical guidelines are followed in receiving, judging, and applying prophecy, its operation will be a blessing in your life and not a source of frustration.

8

Prophetic Clarity

To end our discussion on avoiding the pitfalls of prophetic ministry, we want to answer some common questions regarding the gift of prophecy.

Prophetic Questions & Answers

We have to desire prophetic clarity and purity. If this remains our desire, the Lord will protect us from error and deception. We will avoid the pitfalls of prophetic ministry.

Can someone prophesy at will? The answer to this question is No. When we prophesy, we speak for another. Prophecy comes from God, alone. Though we can stir up the gifts of God on the inside, it is based upon the will of God when prophecy is received and ministered.

Is prophecy the same as preaching? Though there are similar functions between these two ministries, prophecy is not the same as preaching. Preaching is designed to convert men to the knowledge of the truth. Preaching may have prophetic elements, since all of God's word is prophetic, but it is not prophecy in its purest sense.

Prophecy helps men to continue in the truth presented through preaching. Preaching offers a general word for the masses. Conversely, prophecy comes to specific people for specific situations.

If a prophecy is not clear, does it make it invalid? It is true that unclear prophecy may not be from the Lord. However, prophecy does come in part. God may send a seemingly vague prophecy in order to draw the hearer into prayer.

Are all prophecies conditional? Most personal prophecies are conditional. If we remain in Him and serve Him in faith, we will receive what the Lord promised. Prophecies concerning God's eternal purpose are not conditional. They will happen according to His word.

Can someone impart the gift of prophecy to another? Impartation can only take place by the will of God. He is the one who anoints and gives gifts. If He desires for someone to share in the anointing or gift in our life, He will allow an impartation.

This is similar to Him taking Moses' spirit and placing it upon the elders. However, Moses did not do it; it was done by the will of God. If God does not plan for you to have a certain gift or ministry, no men can impart what they have. It has to be in God's will.

Elisha could receive a double portion of

Elijah's spirit because he was to replace him in the prophetic office. His reception of the mantle and double portion were in line with the calling of God upon his life. In these instances, God gives us mentors and spiritual fathers/mothers to impart a portion of themselves into our lives, which will enhance the ministry already in us.

Can someone prophesy without the gift of prophecy? Yes. The Holy Spirit dwells in every believer but manifests Himself differently in each. Since He abides in the believer, He may see fit to use someone in a gift that he does not normally function in for a particular purpose. In addition, when the spirit of prophecy comes in the Church, any believer present will be able to prophesy.

If my parents are prophets and/or have the gift of prophecy, does that make me a prophet? Will I have the gift of prophecy? Not necessarily. The gifts and callings of God are based upon the discretion of the Lord, not family. Though God sometimes uses whole families in similar ministries, it is not the standard.

Is prophecy a gift that one is born with? No. Every spiritual gift is an endowment of the Spirit of the Lord. *Only God can reveal and give gifts and callings that you may have, family ties or natural attributes cannot be used to define them.* *

Remember, the Spirit gives gifts at His own will. Don't use Jeremiah's commission as a basis for this erroneous thought of being born with a spiritual gift. Jeremiah was ordained a prophet before birth and while in the womb. He did not receive a spiritual endowment until the Lord laid His hands on his mouth (Jeremiah 1:9).

Gifts may be imparted at one's new birth in Christ, not at the natural birth. John the Baptist cannot be used as an example either. It was a unique event when he leaped in Elizabeth womb and she was filled with the Spirit and prophesied. He only *leaped,* and *she was filled*; no biblical record state's the baby **had** the Spirit.

Does scripture negate the operation of personal prophecy? No. Even after the Holy Ghost came, and the Church was established, God gave individuals the gift of prophecy. If it was operational then, it still provides a great blessing to the Church today.

Does having the gift of prophecy make me a prophet? No. The gift of prophecy can be in any believer. It may be a sign of a prophetic calling. The prophet's call is more than the gift of prophecy, it is foundational to the Church. God calls them personally to service. If you have not experienced this, you may be called to operate solely in the gift of prophecy or a prophetic anointing.

Can women be called to the office of the prophet?
In the Old Testament, we have record of women
being called to the prophetic office. Women such as
Miriam, Huldah, and Deborah were called
prophetesses.

Since the prophetic ministry continues in the
New Testament Church, then we know that women
are still being called to this office.

*Is the gift of prophecy only concerned with the
future?* No. The gift of prophecy is a 'now' word
from the Lord. It brings us into the mind of God. It
may contain predictive elements, though this is only
a part of the manifestation of the gift of prophecy.

*Can someone be called as a prophet and do not
have the gift of prophecy?* No. This is why a prophet
is called a prophet. His ministry is given to speak
for or prophesy in the name of the Lord. He would
not be able to perform His purpose without the gift

of prophecy. Prophecy is the basis for the prophet's ministry.

If I desire the gift of prophecy, will God give it to me? The scriptures tell us to ask God for the best gifts. He would not have told us to ask, if He did not intend to give us our request. If God denies your request for this gift, trust His wisdom. However, we can ask and expect to receive.

www.ingramcontent.com/pod-product-compliance
Lightning Source LLC
Chambersburg PA
CBHW020514100426
42813CB00030B/3235/J